Busy Woman's Checklists

Susan Tatsui-D'Arcy

PRENTICE HALL
Paramus, New Jersey 07652

Printed in the United States of America

10 9 8 7 6 5 4 3 2 1

ISBN 0-13-639576-7 (p)

ATTENTION: CORPORATIONS AND SCHOOLS

Prentice Hall books are available at quantity discounts with bulk purchase for educational, business, or sales promotional use. For information, please write to: Prentice Hall Special Sales, 240 Frisch Court, Paramus, New Jersey 07652. Please supply: title of book, ISBN, quantity, how the book will be used, date needed.

PRENTICE HALL
Paramus, NJ 07652

A Simon & Schuster Company

On the World Wide Web at http://www.phdirect.com

Prentice Hall International (UK) Limited, *London*
Prentice Hall of Australia Pty. Limited, *Sydney*
Prentice Hall Canada, Inc., *Toronto*
Prentice Hall Hispanoamericana, S.A., *Mexico*
Prentice Hall of India Private Limited, *New Delhi*
Prentice Hall of Japan, Inc., *Tokyo*
Simon & Schuster Asia Pte. Ltd., *Singapore*
Editora Prentice Hall do Brasil, Ltda., *Rio de Janeiro*

Acknowledgments

With grateful acknowledgment to Sybil Grace, who expertly compiled and developed the checklists and nurtured the book throughout its development; and to the following people at Prentice Hall, without whom this book would not have been possible:

Linda Conway, *Art Director*
Christine Wolf, *Interior Designer*
Jackie Roulette, *Production Editor*
Robyn Beckerman, *Desktop Editor*
Audrey Kopciak, *Desktop Editor*

Thanks also to the following individuals who reviewed the manuscript and gave their helpful input: Connie Kallback, Joan-Ellen Messina, and Susan Sherman.

Special thanks to Ellen Schneid Coleman, Executive Editor, who proposed and initiated this project.

Note: "Timesaving Tips for Grooming and Dressing" and "Unexpected Business Trips" were adapted from *The Working Woman's Guide to Managing Time*, Roberta Roesch, Prentice Hall, 1996. "Choose Your Exercise" was adapted from *The Busy Executive's Guide to Total Fitness*, Adele Pace with Maria Jones, Prentice Hall, 1995.

Contents

CONTENTS

Introduction

You are a busy woman; you have many responsibilities—work, home, family. You also want to make time for friends, leisure activities, relaxation. Time is your most valuable asset, and it's the one thing you never have enough of. You need all the help you can get, and *Busy Woman's Checklists* can help. Just keep it handy—in your purse or briefcase—and you'll have valuable assistance and time-savers at your fingertips.

☐ Are you always shopping on the run? You'll have your family's clothing sizes when you need them.

☐ Need to schedule routine car maintenance? You'll have all the information you need to make that appointment.

☐ Forget which bills are due when? Turn to the "Bill-Payment Schedule" and avoid credit snarls.

☐ Planning your child's birthday party? Use the *Checklists* to save time and energy.

☐ Stuck for gift ideas? Turn to "Gift Ideas for Special Occasions" and make your selection!

☐ Need to report breakage or damage to your insurance company? Find the information you need in "Household Inventory."

☐ Suddenly called out of town? You'll be prepared for any business trip with the *Checklists*.

INTRODUCTION

☐ Planning your vacation? Use the "Vacation Checklist" to leave your home secure.

☐ Have an encounter with a rusty nail? Review your immunization record to see whether you need a tetanus shot.

These are just a few examples of how *Busy Woman's Checklists* will help you stay organized in managing your household, your money, and just about every other aspect of your life.

Managing Your Time and Household

I believe one thing: that today is yesterday and tomorrow is today and you can't stop.

MARTHA GRAHAM

Daily Timesavers

Getting Ready for Work

☐ Decide what you're going to wear the night before; get clothing and accessories ready.

☐ If you bring your breakfast or lunch to work, prepare it the night before.

☐ Set aside money for tolls and put it where you can get it quickly in the car.

☐ Keep a "To Bring" list and check it before you leave for work, so you won't forget anything you need for work.

At Work

☐ Check your "To Do" list. Assess priorities and rank tasks in order of importance.

☐ To avoid interruptions, let your telephone callers leave messages—don't pick up your phone.

☐ Check your messages periodically. Establish a schedule; for example, check just before lunch; check in the afternoon; check before you leave the office.

□ Use e-mail and telephone in-house to save steps and get faster results.

□ Prepare the "To Do" list for the next day before you leave the office.

At Home

□ Make lists; plan the week in advance; plan what you'll do each evening.

□ Make a list of all regularly scheduled activities.

□ Keep a family calendar so everyone knows what's scheduled and what's planned.

□ Shop for food once a week. Keep a running list. Also, keep a list of food in your pantry and in your freezer. Note the date of purchase and the date you froze the food.

□ Plan meals ahead for the entire week. Post your menu so everyone knows what's needed and can help get meals on the table.

□ Cook several batches of meals at a time and freeze the extras. (See "Foods that Freeze Well.")

□ Have a central "drop" for the family's dry cleaning. Schedule one trip to the dry cleaner with everyone's clothing. If possible, set up a regular time for this—say, every two weeks.

☐ Set up a regular schedule for doing the laundry: linens and towels one day; clothing another day.

☐ Assign chores to each family member. Post a schedule of what each person is supposed to do and when the chore is supposed to be done.

Personal Timesavers

☐ Shop for clothing no more than once a season— or, if you can, twice a year.

☐ Shop by phone, mail order, as much as possible. Consider doing gift shopping this way.

☐ Schedule important matters, such as regular medical and dental checkups, well in advance. Consider having all the children's examinations one after the other on the same day.

☐ Schedule leisure-time activities. Be sure to set aside time for hobbies, recreation, and entertainment.

☐ Plan vacations well in advance. Request your time off early.

For Children

☐ Get them to choose their school clothing the night before and lay it out.

☐ Have them prepare their lunches the night before.

☐ Make sure they pack their bookbags or carryalls before they go to bed.

☐ School or club notices or memos should be placed in one special place so they can be reviewed and appropriate decisions made. If notices are about activities or meetings, etc., these can then be noted on the calendar.

☐ They should keep a list of supplies—for school/hobbies—and let you know when they run out of something.

☐ Party or play invitations must be discussed as soon as they are received, so they can be added to the calendar if approved.

Foods that Freeze Well

Dinners

Chili
Spaghetti sauce
Meatballs
Enchiladas
Stew
Soups
Chicken Cacciatore

Turkey slices
Turkey Tetrazzini
Frankfurters
Hamburger patties
Lasagna
Macaroni and cheese
Tuna casserole

Other Foods

Bread, rolls, buns
Waffles
Pancakes
Cooked vegetables
Gravies
Stuffing
English muffins
Cakes/cookies
Berries
Cold cuts

Timesaving Tips for Grooming and Dressing

Organize your clothing and makeup to make your daily routine fast, efficient, and hassle-free. You'll look your best in less time, and start the day feeling ready for anything!

Grooming Tips

☐ Keep all your makeup and skin and hair supplies on one tray. You'll save time by not having to hunt for supplies.

☐ Choose a hair style that's easy to care for. If you have long hair, consider wearing it up or back during the work week.

☐ Practice doing your morning routine in 20 minutes or less—10 minutes for your hair and 10 minutes for your makeup.

☐ Get a good, understated natural look with a light makeup application. Use a splash of toner, a little moisturizer and foundation, light blusher, powder, mascara, eye shadow. Apply a lip moisturizer and then your lipstick.

☐ Remove your makeup at the end of the day. Take 10 minutes to wash your face, apply cleansing lotion, toner, and moisturizer or night cream.

Dressing Tips

☐ Hang your clothing so you can find what you need quickly. Hang all suits together, skirts together, pants together, tops together, jackets together.

☐ Decide what you're going to wear the night before and lay it out for quick dressing.

☐ Rotate clothing from front to back (or left to right) so that the clothing you wore most recently is in the back (or other side) of the closet.

☐ If you have two closets, use one for winter clothes and one for summer clothes. Think of all the time you'll save by not having to change closets.

☐ Build your wardrobe on one or two main colors so you can match your clothing and accessories quickly.

☐ Select one or two basic colors for shoes, hand-bags, and accessories to coordinate with your main colors.

☐ Include a basic dress in your wardrobe in a dark or neutral color that you can wear year round. You can dress it up or down with accessories.

☐ Hang your belts and scarves on towel racks attached to the back of your closet door. The scarves will stay neat, and you'll find what you need quickly.

☐ Don't keep what you don't wear. If you haven't worn something in a year, get rid of it.

☐ Save last-minute ironing time by hanging the wrinkled clothing in the bathroom while you shower. The steam from the shower will help smooth the wrinkles.

☐ To free a stuck zipper, run a lead pencil up and down the zipper.

Important Telephone Numbers

Medical

☐ Emergency: _____

☐ Poison control center: _____

☐ Family doctor: _____

☐ Pediatrician:_____

☐ Other: _____

☐ Other: _____

☐ Dentist: _____

☐ Orthodontist: _____

☐ Periodontist:_____

☐ Veterinarian: _____

Child Care

☐ Babysitter: _____

_____

_____

□ Day-care center: _____

□ School: _____

□ School: _____

□ School: _____

□ After-school program: _____

□ After-school program: _____

□ After-school program: _____

Work

□ Office: _____

□ Office—spouse: _____

Household

□ Plumber: _____

□ Carpenter/handyman: _____

□ Electrician: _____

□ Auto mechanic: _____

□ Appliance repair:_____

□ Lawn service: _____

MANAGING YOUR TIME AND HOUSEHOLD

☐ Snow removal: _____
☐ Gas company: _____
☐ Electric company: _____
☐ Oil company: _____
☐ Water company: _____
☐ Chimney sweep: _____
☐ Air conditioning service: _____
☐ Water softener/filter service: _____

Apartment/Condo/Coop

☐ Superintendent: _____
☐ Maintenance office: _____
☐ Rental office: _____
☐ Landlord: _____
☐ Managing agent: _____

Personal

☐ Beauty parlor: _____
☐ Library: _____

☐ Gym/health club: _____

Legal and Financial

☐ Attorney: _____

☐ Accountant: _____

☐ Insurance agent: _____

☐ Financial planner: _____

☐ Stockbroker: _____

Other

☐ Family: _____

_____

_____

_____

_____

_____

_____

_____

_____

MANAGING YOUR TIME AND HOUSEHOLD

☐ Friends: _____

_____

_____

_____

_____

_____

☐ Neighbors: _____

_____

_____

_____

_____

☐ Other: _____

_____

_____

_____

_____

_____

The Busy Shopper

Fill in the names, telephone numbers, and hours of operation of the stores you shop in regularly. You'll find having this information at hand a real time-saver!

☐ Supermarket: _____

_____

_____

_____

☐ Pharmacy: _____

☐ Convenience store: _____

☐ Hardware store: _____

☐ Stationery store: _____

☐ Shoe repair shop: _____

☐ Dry cleaner: _____

☐ Video rental store: _____

☐ Children's clothing store: _____

_____

MANAGING YOUR TIME AND HOUSEHOLD

☐ Shoe store: _____

☐ Toy store: _____

☐ Music store: _____

☐ Book store: _____

☐ Department stores: _____

_____

_____

_____

_____

☐ Specialty shops: _____

_____

_____

_____

_____

☐ Other: _____

_____

_____

_____

Car-Maintenance Schedule

Car 1

☐ Annual inspection date: _____

☐ Tires rotated: _____

☐ Next rotation: _____

☐ Oil changed: _____

☐ Next oil change: _____

☐ Tuneup: _____

☐ Next tuneup: _____

☐ Brake fluid checked: _____

☐ Transmission fluid checked: _____

☐ Next fluids check: _____

☐ Antifreeze checked:_____

☐ Next check: _____

☐ Hoses checked: _____

☐ Next check: _____

Car 2

☐ Annual inspection date: _____

☐ Tires rotated: _____

☐ Next rotation: _____

☐ Oil changed: _____

☐ Next oil change: _____

☐ Tuneup: _____

☐ Next tuneup: _____

☐ Brake fluid checked: _____

☐ Transmission fluid checked: _____

☐ Next fluids check: _____

☐ Antifreeze checked: _____

☐ Next check: _____

☐ Hoses checked: _____

☐ Next check: _____

Home-Maintenance Checklist ✐

If You Own Your Own Home

☐ Have your roof checked for loose shingles, flashing. Clean off debris. Note age of roof: _____. Roof replaced _____.

☐ Have your gutters checked. Make sure there are no leaks or corroded material. Have gutters cleaned of debris.

☐ Have downspouts flushed to make sure they are not clogged.

☐ Have the chimney checked and cleaned; make sure the flue is not clogged. Make sure there are no cracks.

☐ Have the exterior of the house checked for broken or damaged shingles; cracked siding, damaged brick, etc.

☐ Have all wood trim checked for rot, mildew, damage, peeling paint. Wash exterior to get rid of mildew and dirt. Paint as needed.

☐ House was painted in _____. Paint color/company: _____.

☐ Have all windows inspected—check caulking; make sure glass is not blemished or cracked; check sashes and wooden trim.

☐ Have doors checked. Make sure weatherstripping is in good condition and hinges are oiled; for the fall, make sure storm doors are operating correctly; clean storm panels. For the spring, store storm panels; clean and install screen panels.

☐ Have stoops examined for crumbling cement, cracked steps, dried out or missing mortar.

☐ Have patio/porch checked for cracks, leaks, damage.

☐ Have garage inspected; clean and sweep.

☐ Inspect all tools and equipment such as snow blower, lawn mower, mulcher, and so on; oil and get ready for seasonal use.

☐ Have basement checked for cracks in foundation, water, or other damage. Make sure all basement windows are in good condition.

☐ Check central (or wall/window) air-conditioning unit. Clean or replace filters.

☐ Have attic checked for signs of animal infestation or moisture or mildew damage.

☐ Have fireplace and chimney thoroughly swept out and checked. Make sure the flue is cleaned.

☐ Check water softener. Make sure your softener supply is adequate and the system is functioning properly. Check the filter.

☐ Check for any insect infestation around the house, in the garage, basement, or attic. Make sure you use a licensed exterminator to get rid of any problems.

☐ Check smoke alarms and fire extinguishers. Replace old batteries and refill extinguishers.

If You Own an Apartment/Condo/Coop

☐ Check walls, ceilings for peeling paint, cracks. Apartment was painted in _____; due to be painted in _____.

☐ Check floors; wood floors may need to be refinished.

☐ Check door(s) to make sure weatherstripping is in good condition and that hinges are oiled.

☐ Check windows for leaks and cracks.

☐ Have air conditioning units checked; have filters cleaned or replaced.

If You Rent an Apartment/Condo/Coop

☐ Make sure painting schedule is maintained.
Apartment was painted in _____;
due to be painted in _____.

☐ Make sure floors are in good condition.

☐ Check doors to make sure weatherstripping
is in good condition and that hinges operate
smoothly.

☐ Make sure window-
cleaning schedule
is maintained. Also
have windows
checked for leaks,
cracks. Have
storms /screens
installed.

☐ Make sure extermi-
nator's schedule is
maintained.

Notes

Managing
Your
Money

The most popular labor-saving device is still money.

PHYLLIS GEORGE

Budgeting for the Month

Item	Monthly Expense
HOUSEHOLD	
Food	_____
Rent/mortgage	_____
Electricity	_____
Heat: gas/oil	_____
Water	_____
Trash/garbage service	_____
Snow removal	_____
Lawn service	_____
Insurance	_____
Telephone	_____
Cleaning help	_____
Child care	_____
Cable TV	_____
Other	_____
Total:	_____

Item	Monthly Expense
PERSONAL EXPENSES	
General allowance	_____
Commuting costs	_____
Gasoline	_____
Gifts	_____
Lunches	_____
Clothes	_____
Dry cleaning	_____
Beauty salon/Barber	_____
Movies	_____
Theater	_____
Dinners out	_____
Membership dues	_____
Newspapers	_____
Magazines	_____
Sports/related activities	_____
Other	_____
Total:	_____

MANAGING YOUR MONEY

Item	Monthly Expense
EDUCATION	
Tuition	_____
Board	_____
Supplies	_____
Other	_____
Other	_____
Total:	_____
INSURANCE	
Homeowner's	_____
Renter's	_____
Health	_____
Automobile	_____
Life	_____
Other	_____
Other	_____
Total:	_____

Item	Monthly Expense
Financial Expenses	
Auto loan	_____
Home-equity loan	_____
Other bank loans	_____
Credit card purchases	_____
Other	_____
Other	_____
Total:	_____
Grand Total:	_____

Credit Management ━━

Credit Card _____
Card number: _____
Expiration date: _____
Emergency phone number: _____

Credit Card _____
Card number: _____
Expiration date: _____
Emergency phone number: _____

Credit Card _____
Card number: _____
Expiration date: _____
Emergency phone number: _____

Credit Card _____
Card number: _____
Expiration date: _____
Emergency phone number: _____

Credit Card _____
Card number: _____
Expiration date: _____
Emergency phone number: _____

Credit Card _____

Card number: _____

Expiration date: _____

Emergency phone number: _____

Credit Card _____

Card number: _____

Expiration date: _____

Emergency phone number: _____

Credit Card _____

Card number: _____

Expiration date: _____

Emergency phone number: _____

Bank _____

Phone number: _____

Hours open: _____

Bank _____

Phone number: _____

Hours open: _____

Bank _____

Phone number: _____

Hours open: _____

Bill-Payment Schedule

☐ Mortgage: _____

☐ Estimated-tax: _____

☐ Gas and electricity: _____

_____

☐ Water: _____

☐ Telephone: _____

_____

☐ Cellular phone: _____

_____

☐ Cable TV: _____

☐ Car: _____

_____

☐ Automobile insurance: _____

_____

☐ Homeowner's insurance: _____

☐ Renter's insurance: _____

- ☐ Health insurance:_____
- ☐ Life insurance:_____

_____

- ☐ School tuition: _____

_____

- ☐ Music lessons: _____
- ☐ Dancing lessons: _____
- ☐ Gym/Health club: _____

_____

- ☐ Spa: _____
- ☐ Martial Arts: _____
- ☐ Tennis:_____
- ☐ Golf:_____
- ☐ Swimming lessons: _____
- ☐ Organization dues: _____

_____

_____

_____

33

MANAGING YOUR MONEY

☐ Store: _____ : _____

_____ : _____

_____ : _____

_____ : _____

☐ Loan: _____ : _____

_____ : _____

☐ Other: _____

_____

_____

_____

_____

Notes

Managing
Your
Life

It's not what you do once in a while,
It's what you do day in and day out
That makes the difference.

JENNY CRAIG

Relaxation Techniques for Managing Stress

Being busy and constantly on the go can be extremely stressful. Stress can slow you down, sometimes immobilize you, and prevent you from functioning efficiently. You need to relax to eliminate stress. You'll be amazed at the difference these relaxation techniques will make in your life. You'll feel better and find yourself working smarter and with more energy. Best of all, you'll learn how to control stress.

At Work

☐ Take a breather. While sitting at your desk, take a break. Clear your mind. Close your eyes. Breathe deeply for a few minutes. Breathe out; count to 12. Breathe in; count to 12. Repeat at least five times. Concentrate on relaxing; don't think of anything else.

☐ Exercise is an excellent relaxer. You can do the following exercises to stretch your arms and legs while sitting at your desk.

— Hold your arms out at your sides. Make circles; first, one arm at a time; then, both arms together.

— Hold your arms out in front of you. Lift them up; first, one at a time; then, both together.

— Do each move for 8 counts.

— Lift your legs under the desk; hold them straight out for 8 counts. Then, put them down for 8 counts. Repeat at least five times.

— Rotate your head to loosen neck muscles.

You'll find that even a few minutes of these simple exercises will make a difference.

☐ Walk as much as possible. Hand-deliver work to your co-workers, instead of using the interoffice mail. Use the stairs instead of the elevator. Park farther away from the building entrance. Don't use the nearest restroom; use one that requires a short walk. As you walk, breathe deeply and clear your mind.

☐ Have a pleasant aroma in your office. A small dish of potpourri or sachet in your favorite scent will make you feel more relaxed.

☐ Have soothing teas on hand to calm you when you are upset and stressed. Peppermint tea is very soothing. There are many other teas and blends available to relax you. Visit the specialty

39

foods aisle of your supermarket or your health-food store.

☐ Take the time to enjoy a well-balanced lunch. Avoid junk foods, excess sweets, eating "on the run." Don't cram other activities into your lunch hour.

☐ If you bring lunch from home, take a short walk outside to get fresh air. Try not to eat lunch at your desk; have your lunch in a lounge or other room.

☐ Prioritize your "To Do" list. Be realistic in setting daily goals and build in time for interruptions. On days when there are no interruptions, you'll be able to accomplish the next task on your list.

At Home

☐ When you come home from work, don't rush right into the family activities. Establish a "time-out" routine. Take a break of at least 10 to 20 minutes. Change your clothes. Lie down or just sit quietly to unwind. Listen to soothing music.

☐ Weather and time permitting, take a walk around your neighborhood or in the nearest park. You might prefer to do this after dinner, depending on the season of the year.

☐ Enjoy a well-balanced dinner with the family. Have everyone pitch in to help get dinner ready and on the table. Have everyone share the after-dinner cleanup chores.

☐ Rest after dinner. This is a good time to read the newspaper or watch TV.

☐ After a stressful or strenuous day, take a soothing warm bath. Add bath salts, bath gels, or a similar item in your favorite scent.

☐ Include some physical activity in your life. Select an athletic activity—bowling, tennis, swimming, or an exercise class. Sign up for tai chi, karate, or dancing. Join a health club. You'll be amazed at how relaxed you'll feel after your activity.

Choose Your Exercise!

Staying fit makes you feel better, more in control, and better organized. Here is an easy way to compare the benefits of a variety of exercises; choose the ones that are right for you.

Exercise	Cardiovascular Benefit	Muscular Benefit	Convenience	Equipment Affordability	Injury Safe
Walking:					
indoors	++	+	++++	+	++++
outdoors	++	+	+++	++++	++++
Running:					
indoors	++++	++	++++	+	+++
outdoors	++++	++	+++	++++	++
Cross country skiing	++++	++	++++	++	++++

Exercise					
Cycling: stationary bike	++++	++	++++	++	++++
bicycle	++++	++	++	+	+++
Aerobics	++++	++	++	+++	++
Stairclimbing	++++	++	++++	+	+++
Rowing	+++	++	++++	+	++
Swimming	++	++	+	+++	++++
Push-ups	+	+++	++++	++++	+++
Sit-ups	+	+++	++++	++++	++++

Key: + = poor   ++ = average   +++ = good   ++++ = excellent

Adult-Activities Schedule

This will help you keep track of your and your spouse's activities. Make sure you jot them down on the family calendar too.

Me

Day/time	Activity

Spouse

Day/time	Activity

Party-Planning Checklist

☐ Choose the date.

☐ Book the restaurant/hall/room if not at your home.

☐ Make up the guest list.

☐ Send invitations.

☐ Keep a record of responses so you have an accurate head count.

☐ Select/plan the menu.

☐ Hire cooking/serving help or select a caterer.

☐ Rent equipment—extra chairs/tables/dinnerware/flatware/glasses/table linens/cooking utensils.

☐ Shop for food.

☐ If you are cooking yourself, cook ahead and freeze.

☐ Shop for beverages—soda/beer/wine/liquor.

☐ Set up tables; set up bar.

☐ Review meal and drink plans with servers.

☐ Enjoy the party!

Party-Planning Notes

Gift Ideas for Special Occasions

When you need a special gift idea, start your search here. You'll save a lot of time and energy.

High School Graduation

Alarm clock
Hot pot—electric pot that boils water for soup,
    coffee, tea
Dorm linens, towels
Luggage
Reference books—dictionary, thesaurus

College Graduation

Fountain pen-and-pencil set
Briefcase/portfolio
Luggage
Electronic organizer
Business-card case

End-of-School/Holiday Gifts for Teachers

Stationery
Scented candles
Hand-lotion/body-lotion gift basket
Gift certificate for dinner at a local restaurant
Gift certificate for a local movie theater

Engagement

Vase
Candy dish/biscuit barrel
Picture frame
Cake plate and server
Crystal bowl

Bridal Shower

Gift certificate for facial, manicure, pedicure
Small appliances—coffee grinder, toaster
Coffee maker/teapot with infuser
Specialized cooking items—electric pepper mill,
   garlic baker, stovetop grill pan, pizza stone
Cookbook

Wedding—aside from money or items selected from a bridal registry

Candlesticks
Camcorder
VCR or television set
Microwave oven
Gas grill

Wedding Anniversary

Tickets for the theater or other cultural events
Gift certificate to a restaurant

The above are appropriate for a first-anniversary (paper) gift, too.

Use the list below to select appropriate gifts. Some specific suggestions follow.

Year	Traditional	Modern
1	Paper	Clock
2	Cotton	China
3	Leather	Crystal, glass
4	Flowers	Electrical appliance
5	Wool	Silverware
6	Candy, iron	Wood
7	Copper, wood	Desk set
8	Bronze, pottery	Linens
9	Pottery, willow	Leather
10	Tin, aluminum	Diamond jewelry
11	Steel	Fashion jewelry
12	Silk, linen	Pearl
13	Lace	Textiles, furs
14	Ivory	Gold jewelry
15	Crystal	Watches

20	China	Platinum
25	Silver	Silver
30	Pearl	Diamond
35	Coral	Jade
40	Ruby	Ruby
45	Sapphire	Sapphire
50	Gold	Gold
55	Emerald	Emerald
60	Diamond	Diamond
75	Diamond	Diamond

Cotton—place mats, tablecloth, napkins

Leather—his-and-hers eyeglass/sunglass cases

Wood—handcrafted breadboard, picture frame

Iron—wrought-iron candleholders

Copper—planter, jewelry/pin for her/tie tack for him

Bronze—paperweight, small sculpture

Pottery—serving platter, tea set, garlic keeper

Tin—toleware item/decorative box, holder for fire-place matches

Baby Shower

Diaper bag
Basket of assorted baby needs—diapers/bottles/baby
  soap/baby powder, etc.
Picture frame
Photo album
Layette items—infant-size onesies, stretchies,
  receiving blankets, hooded towels

New Baby

Journal to record baby's first year
Activity mat
Diaper compactor
Folding travel stroller
Folding travel crib/playpen

Mother's Day

Gift certificate for facial, manicure, pedicure
Spa weekend
Theater tickets
Magazine subscription
Framed picture of children/grandchildren

Father's Day

Tickets to sports event, cultural event
Magazine subscription
Sports or hobby equipment
Clothing—sports shirt/athletic gear
Gift certificate for CDs, tapes

Christening

Savings bond/money
Bible
Jewelry—cross

Communion/Confirmation

Money
Fountain pen
Jewelry

Bar Mitzvah

Savings bond/money
Gift certificate to a bookstore
Fountain pen

Bat Mitzvah

Savings bond/money
Jewelry
Jewelry box

Child's Birthday

Videos—children's movies, CDs, tapes
Toys—hobby equipment
Clothing

Adult's Birthday

Personalized notes/stationery
Scarf—woman; tie—man
Gift certificate to music store or bookstore

53

Use the list below of birthstones and flowers for appropriate birthday gifts of jewelry or flowers.

Month	Old-Fashioned Stone	Modern Stone	Flower
January	Garnet	Garnet	Carnation
February	Amethyst	Amethyst	Violet
March	Jasper	Bloodstone or Aquamarine	Jonquil
April	Sapphire	Diamond	Sweet Pea
May	Agate	Emerald	Lily of the Valley
June	Emerald	Pearl, Moonstone, or Alexandrite	Rose
July	Onyx	Ruby	Larkspur
August	Carnelian	Sardonyx or Peridot	Gladiolus
September	Chrysolite	Sapphire	Aster
October	Aquamarine	Opal or Tourmaline	Calendula
November	Topaz	Topaz	Chrysanthemum
December	Ruby	Turquoise or Zircon	Narcissus

General Gift Note: Books make excellent gifts, and they're always the right size and color. Consider giving books for new-baby gifts as well as for birthdays and other special occasions.

Gift Record

Here's an easy way to keep track of the gifts that you give. You won't run the risk of forgetting what you gave last time and giving the same gift twice.

Name: _____

Gift: _____

Date: _____ Cost: _____

Occasion: _____

Name: _____

Gift: _____

Date: _____ Cost: _____

Occasion: _____

Name: _____

Gift: _____

Date: _____ Cost: _____

Occasion: _____

Name: _____

Gift: _____

Date: _____ Cost: _____

Occasion: _____

Name: _____

Gift: _____

Date: _____ Cost: _____

Occasion: _____

Name: _____

Gift: _____

Date: _____ Cost: _____

Occasion: _____

Name: _____

Gift: _____

Date: _____ Cost: _____

Occasion: _____

Name: _____

Gift: _____

Date: _____ Cost: _____

Occasion: _____

Name: _____

Gift: _____

Date: _____ Cost: _____

Occasion: _____

Name: _____

Gift: _____

Date: _____ Cost: _____

Occasion: _____

Name: _____

Gift: _____

Date: _____ Cost: _____

Occasion: _____

Name: _____

Gift: _____

Date: _____ Cost: _____

Occasion: _____

Name: _____

Gift: _____

Date: _____ Cost: _____

Occasion: _____

Clothing Sizes

In addition to recording sizes, it's a good idea to make a note of preferred or needed colors.

Spouse

☐ Underwear: _____

☐ Socks: _____

☐ Shirts—Neck: _____ Sleeve: _____

☐ Pajamas: _____

☐ Robe: _____

☐ Slacks: _____

☐ Belt: _____

☐ Jacket: _____

☐ Coat: _____

☐ Suit: _____

☐ Jeans: _____

☐ Tee shirts/polo shirts: _____

☐ Shoes: _____

☐ Boots: _____

☐ Slippers: _____

Other family member: _____

☐ Underwear: _____

☐ Socks: _____

☐ Shirts—Neck: _____Sleeve: _____

☐ Pajamas: _____

☐ Robe: _____

☐ Slacks: _____

☐ Belt: _____

☐ Jacket: _____

☐ Coat: _____

☐ Suit: _____

☐ Jeans: _____

☐ Tee shirts/polo shirts: _____

☐ Shoes: _____

☐ Boots: _____

☐ Slippers: _____

Other family member: _____

☐ Underwear: _____

☐ Socks: _____

☐ Shirts—Neck: _____Sleeve: _____

☐ Pajamas: _____

☐ Robe: _____

☐ Slacks: _____

☐ Belt: _____

☐ Jacket: _____

☐ Coat: _____

☐ Suit: _____

☐ Jeans: _____

☐ Tee shirts/polo shirts: _____

☐ Shoes: _____

☐ Boots: _____

☐ Slippers: _____

Other family member: _____

☐ Underwear: _____

☐ Socks: _____

☐ Shirts—Neck: _____ Sleeve: _____

☐ Pajamas: _____

☐ Robe: _____

☐ Slacks: _____

☐ Belt: _____

☐ Jacket: _____

☐ Coat: _____

☐ Suit: _____

☐ Jeans: _____

☐ Tee shirts/polo shirts: _____

☐ Shoes: _____

☐ Boots: _____

☐ Slippers: _____

Other family member: _____

☐ Underwear: _____

☐ Socks: _____

☐ Shirts—Neck: _____ Sleeve: _____

☐ Pajamas: _____

☐ Robe: _____

☐ Slacks: _____

☐ Belt: _____

☐ Jacket: _____

☐ Coat: _____

☐ Suit: _____

☐ Jeans: _____

☐ Tee shirts/polo shirts: _____

☐ Shoes: _____

☐ Boots: _____

☐ Slippers: _____

Other family member: _____

☐ Underwear: _____

☐ Socks: _____

☐ Shirts—Neck: _____Sleeve: _____

☐ Pajamas: _____

☐ Robe: _____

☐ Slacks: _____

☐ Belt: _____

☐ Jacket: _____

☐ Coat: _____

☐ Suit: _____

☐ Jeans: _____

☐ Tee shirts/polo shirts: _____

☐ Shoes: _____

☐ Boots: _____

☐ Slippers: _____

Other family member: _____

☐ Underwear: _____

☐ Socks: _____

☐ Shirts—Neck: _____ Sleeve: _____

☐ Pajamas: _____

☐ Robe: _____

☐ Slacks: _____

☐ Belt: _____

☐ Jacket: _____

☐ Coat: _____

☐ Suit: _____

☐ Jeans: _____

☐ Tee shirts/polo shirts: _____

☐ Shoes: _____

☐ Boots: _____

☐ Slippers: _____

Other family member: _____

☐ Underwear: _____

☐ Socks: _____

☐ Shirts—Neck: _____ Sleeve: _____

☐ Pajamas: _____

☐ Robe: _____

☐ Slacks: _____

☐ Belt: _____

☐ Jacket: _____

☐ Coat: _____

☐ Suit: _____

☐ Jeans: _____

☐ Tee shirts/polo shirts: _____

☐ Shoes: _____

☐ Boots: _____

☐ Slippers: _____

Other family member: _____

☐ Underwear: _____

☐ Socks: _____

☐ Shirts—Neck: _____ Sleeve: _____

☐ Pajamas: _____

☐ Robe: _____

☐ Slacks: _____

☐ Belt: _____

☐ Jacket: _____

☐ Coat: _____

☐ Suit: _____

☐ Jeans: _____

☐ Tee shirts/polo shirts: _____

☐ Shoes: _____

☐ Boots: _____

☐ Slippers: _____

Notes

Kid
Stuff

*Cleaning your house while your kids are still
growing is like shoveling the walk before it
stops snowing.*

PHYLLIS DILLER

Children's Activities Schedule

Here's a handy way to keep track of all your children's activities. List all sports, clubs, music lessons, art classes, religious programs, and so forth, with their scheduled times. Be sure to mark these on the family calendar at home.

Name: _____

Day/time	Activity

Name: _____

Day/time	*Activity*

Name: _____

Day/time	*Activity*

KID STUFF

Name: _____

Day/time	*Activity*

Name: _____

Day/time	*Activity*

72

Planning a Child's Birthday Party

☐ Choose the date.

☐ Make up the guest list.

☐ If you are planning to have the party outside your home, choose and book the site, for example, a bowling alley, children's activity center, fast-food restaurant party room.

☐ If the party is to be at home, hire or rent entertainment if desired—clown, magician, pony ride, moonwalk or similar equipment.

☐ Involve the child in making or buying invitations.

☐ Send invitations. Make sure to include an ending time for the party.

☐ Hire a helper, if possible.

☐ Plan the menu. Remember to keep it simple; plan for easy-to-serve finger foods.

☐ Order the birthday cake.

☐ Shop for food.

☐ Make up a party-goods shopping list—balloons, streamers, party hats, paper plates, napkins, cups, plastic ware.

☐ If you plan to offer party favors, have the child help select them.

☐ Shop for the party goods and party favors. Don't forget the birthday candles!

☐ Make up the party-favor bags, if you are offering more than one item. Have the child help. Put each guest's name on a bag.

☐ Set up a party agenda—schedule time for all activities and games, as well as for serving the food.

☐ Set up the table.

☐ Follow your schedule.

☐ Happy birthday!

Notes for Planning a Child's Birthday Party

Children's Clothing Sizes

Children grow so quickly, you'll want to use pencil to fill in this list. If the child has a color preference, this is a good place to note that as well.

Name: _____

☐ Underwear: _____

☐ Socks: _____

☐ Shirt/blouse: _____

☐ Belt: _____

☐ Pants: _____

☐ Jeans: _____

☐ Skirt: _____

☐ Dress: _____

☐ Jacket: _____

☐ Coat: _____

☐ Hat/cap: _____

☐ Pajamas: _____

☐ Robe: _____

☐ Bathing suit: _____

☐ Shorts: _____

☐ Tee shirts/polo shirts: _____

_____

☐ Shoes: _____

☐ Sneakers: _____

☐ Slippers: _____

☐ Boots: _____

Name: _____

☐ Underwear: _____

☐ Socks: _____

☐ Shirt/blouse: _____

☐ Belt: _____

☐ Pants: _____

☐ Jeans: _____

☐ Skirt: _____

☐ Dress: _____

☐ Jacket: _____

KID STUFF

☐ Coat: _____

☐ Hat/cap: _____

☐ Pajamas: _____

☐ Robe: _____

☐ Bathing suit: _____

☐ Shorts: _____

☐ Tee shirts/polo shirts: _____

_____

☐ Shoes: _____

☐ Sneakers: _____

☐ Slippers: _____

☐ Boots: _____

Name: _____

☐ Underwear: _____

☐ Socks: _____

☐ Shirt/blouse: _____

☐ Belt: _____

☐ Pants: _____

☐ Jeans: _____

☐ Skirt: _____

☐ Dress: _____

☐ Jacket: _____

☐ Coat: _____

☐ Hat/cap: _____

☐ Pajamas: _____

☐ Robe: _____

☐ Bathing suit: _____

☐ Shorts: _____

☐ Tee shirts/polo shirts: _____

_____

☐ Shoes: _____

☐ Sneakers: _____

☐ Slippers: _____

☐ Boots: _____

Name: _____

☐ Underwear: _____

☐ Socks: _____

☐ Shirt/blouse: _____

KID STUFF

☐ Belt: _____

☐ Pants: _____

☐ Jeans: _____

☐ Skirt: _____

☐ Dress: _____

☐ Jacket: _____

☐ Coat: _____

☐ Hat/cap: _____

☐ Pajamas: _____

☐ Robe: _____

☐ Bathing suit: _____

☐ Shorts: _____

☐ Tee shirts/polo shirts: _____

_____

☐ Shoes: _____

☐ Sneakers: _____

☐ Slippers: _____

☐ Boots: _____

School Dormitory Equipment Checklist ✏

Whether your child attends a boarding school or college or university, you'll find this equipment list helpful in preparing for the school year.

General Room Equipment

☐ Desk lamp: Make sure it gives off a bright light and is safe. (Be wary of halogen lamps; they may overheat, tip over, and cause fires. If you do choose a halogen lamp, make sure it has a sturdy base, uses no more than 300-watt bulb, and has a safety shield.)

☐ Electrical appliances: Be sure to check if students are permitted to have small electrical appliances in the room; for example, hot pots for boiling water for hot drinks and soups; popcorn makers; irons; small microwave ovens.

☐ Waste basket: Get one that's lightweight, easy-to-clean, and has a cover. Make sure to suggest using plastic bags as liners.

☐ Storage bins: Plastic interlocking crates make very good storage bins. They come in different colors, and can brighten a room. They also make it easy for the busy student to keep a room neat, and to find things easily.

☐ Light bulbs: Overhead lights—if they are there at all—tend to be dim. Bring light bulbs of sufficient wattage to brighten up the room.

☐ Hangers: Bring a good supply of hangers. Good sturdy plastic ones will last through the school years, and beyond.

☐ Alarm clock or clock/radio: It's easy to forget this. Make sure you don't!

Bed and Bath

☐ Bed linens: Find out what size sheets you need before you buy linens; many dorms have overly long beds. Take along at least two complete sets of sheets and pillowcases; a pillow; two blankets (depending on the climate); and a bedspread; or a comforter that serves as a blanket and a bedspread.

☐ Towels: Bring at least four bath towels, four hand towels, four washcloths (if your child uses them). Include two beach towels (depending on the location of the school and its gym facilities).

☐ Bath accessories: Buy a shower/bath caddy to hold all essentials—soap, toothbrush, toothpaste, shower cap, shower sponge or washcloth, shampoo, hair conditioner, razor, shaving lotion or cream, deodorant, body powder, lotion, and such.

☐ Laundry bag/basket: Include a large-sized bottle or box of laundry detergent. Your child will appreciate having it at hand.

☐ General tip: Make sure to put your child's name on all belongings.

Extras

☐ Cassette tape player and tapes: If possible, try to find out what equipment your child's roommate is planning to bring, so you don't have duplicate equipment.

☐ CD player and disks: Same as above.

☐ TV set: It's usually better not to have a TV in the room. Most dorms have TV lounges.

☐ Mini refrigerator: If the school permits this in the room, you can always rent one on campus.

□ Computer: Be sure there is accurate wiring
to accommodate a computer and/or computer
accessories. Check with the school. Many
offer students the opportunity to purchase
computer equipment at a special price; to log
on to a school-wide network, and to use
school-subsidized printers (Of course, you
should shop around for the best deals. Also
consider a laptop—it's compact and very
convenient to use.)

Notes

Recordkeeping

Everything is data. But data isn't everything.

PAULINE BART

Important Documents

- ☐ Birth certificates
- ☐ Marriage certificate
- ☐ Passports
- ☐ Deed to home
- ☐ Mortgage
- ☐ Home insurance
- ☐ Health-care papers
- ☐ Life insurance
- ☐ Car title/certificate of ownership
- ☐ Car insurance
- ☐ Bank CDs
- ☐ Stock certificates
- ☐ Bonds
- ☐ Savings bonds
- ☐ Wills
- ☐ Power-of-attorney papers
- ☐ Citizenship papers
- ☐ Loan agreement

- ☐ Tax records—local
- ☐ Tax records—state
- ☐ Tax records—federal
- ☐ Contracts
- ☐ Agreements

☐ _____

☐ _____

☐ _____

☐ _____

☐ _____

☐ _____

Receipts You May Need for Tax Purposes

Be sure to keep all receipts for purchases or services that may be factored into your tax return. Use an accordion file (expanding file) to organize your receipts so it is easy to find them during tax season.

Real Estate
House/condo/coop

Vacation home

Mobile home/trailer

Land

Medical/Dental Expenses Not Covered by Your Health Plan
General checkups

Medical tests

Prescriptions

Medical equipment (for example, wheelchair, surgical hose)

Prosthetic devices

Contact lenses

Eyeglasses

Hearing aids

Orthodontic devices

Dental/periodontal cleaning

Dental/periodontal treatments

Podiatric examinations

Podiatric treatments

Orthotic devices

Chiropractic treatment

Alternative medicine

Home Office

Furniture

Equipment (computer/on-line service)

Utilities (heat, electricity)

Supplies

Business Expenses Not Covered by Your Company

Travel

Entertainment

Professional journals/publications

Dues for professional organizations
Tuition for job-related courses/seminars
Moving expenses
Auto mileage for job-related car use
Other (for example, uniforms)

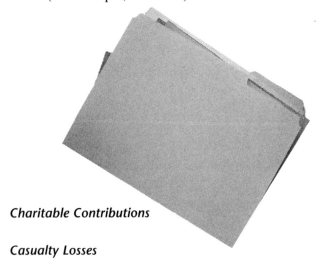

Charitable Contributions

Casualty Losses
Storm damage
Flood-related damage
Fire
Theft

Birthday/Anniversary List

Jot down gift ideas or special interests after each name. (See "Gift Ideas for Special Occasions" on page 48.) Use the "Gift Record" on page 55 to note what gift you gave last year, so you won't inadvertently repeat a gift.

January

_____
_____
_____
_____
_____
_____

February

_____
_____
_____
_____
_____
_____

RECORDKEEPING

March

_____
_____
_____
_____
_____
_____

April

_____
_____
_____
_____
_____
_____

May

_____
_____
_____
_____
_____
_____

June

_____
_____
_____
_____
_____
_____

July

_____
_____
_____
_____
_____
_____

August

_____
_____
_____
_____
_____
_____

RECORDKEEPING

September

_____
_____
_____
_____
_____
_____

October

_____
_____
_____
_____
_____
_____

November

_____
_____
_____
_____
_____
_____

December

_____
_____
_____
_____
_____
_____
_____
_____
_____
_____

Household Inventory

Keep a detailed record of the contents of every room. Note each item, any serial number or identifying number, purchase price, and value. Make a video or take photographs of everything and keep the video or photos with your detailed record in a safety-deposit box. In case of fire or theft, you will be able to document your losses and file claims more efficiently.

Living Room

Antiques/collectibles/art: _____

_____

_____

Carpet/rugs: _____

Sofa/couch: _____

Bookcases: _____

Books: _____

_____

_____

Tables: _____

Chairs: _____

Lamps: _____

Mirrors/Accessories: _____

Stereos/TVs/VCRs: _____

Window shades/drapes/blinds: _____

Miscellaneous: _____

_____

_____

_____

Dining Room

Table: _____

Chairs: _____

China: _____

Silverware: _____

Table linens: _____

Antiques/collectibles/art: _____

Carpet/rugs: _____

Chandelier: _____

Window shades/drapes/blinds: _____

Kitchen

Refrigerator: _____

Stove/microwave: _____

Dishwasher: _____

Lighting: _____

RECORDKEEPING

Appliances: _____

_____

_____

Dishes: _____

Flatware: _____

Cooking utensils/pots/pans:_____

Family Room/Den

Sofa/couch: _____

Tables: _____

Carpet/rugs: _____

Fireplace accessories: _____

Entertainment equipment: _____

Lamps: _____

Window shades/blinds/drapes: _____

Miscellaneous:_____

_____

_____

Master Bedroom

Bed: _____

_____

Night tables:_____

_____

Lamps: _____

_____

Bed linens: _____

_____

Towels/bath accessories: _____

_____

Desks: _____

_____

Miscellaneous: _____

_____

_____

Bedroom

Bed: _____

_____

Night tables:_____

_____

Lamps: _____

_____

Bed linens: _____

_____

Desks: _____

_____

RECORDKEEPING

Miscellaneous: _____

_____

_____

Bedroom

Beds: _____

_____

Night tables: _____

_____

Lamps: _____

_____

Bed linens: _____

_____

Desks: _____

_____

Miscellaneous: _____

_____

_____

Bedroom

Bed: _____

_____

Night tables: _____

_____

Lamps: _____

_____

Bed linens: _____

_____

Desks: _____

_____

Miscellaneous: _____

_____

_____

Laundry Room/Storage/Garage

Washing machine: _____

Dryer: _____

Vacuum cleaner: _____

Sewing machine: _____

Tools: _____

_____

_____

Lawn mower: _____

Mulcher/shredder/edger: _____

Luggage: _____

Outdoor furniture: _____

Miscellaneous: _____

_____

Notes

Travel and Vacation Planning

For years, my husband and I have advocated separate vacations. But the kids keep finding us.

ERMA BOMBECK

Unexpected Business Trips

Don't panic when you are given short notice that you need to travel. You'll always be prepared to go at a moment's notice when you follow these tips.

☐ Have a carry-on suitcase packed and a wardrobe planned and ready at all times.

☐ Keep a cosmetic bag packed with small sizes of your toiletries and cosmetics and a hair dryer and hair-care supplies in the suitcase, along with an extra pair of comfortable shoes, panty-hose, underwear, sleepwear, travel iron, and paperback book.

☐ In the back of your closet hang a good winter or summer nonwrinkle suit fresh from the cleaners that's ready to go into your packed suitcase. You can change the look of the suit daily with scarves, easy-to-pack nonwrinkle tops and pants, and a wool or cotton sweater, depending on the season.

☐ Choose one neutral color for all your business travel, including shoes and purse.

- ☐ Use the large purse you carry to work every day for many of your trip necessities—tickets, travel documents, medications, glasses, jewelry.

- ☐ Make a list of people who can take over for you at home while you're gone. Also, have people at work who can help out so you don't have too much catching up to do when you return.

- ☐ Keep a master list of your household routine that you can post on the refrigerator if someone outside your family will take over while you're away.

- ☐ Have a week's supply of "Only for Emergency" staples and dinners stored in your freezer and cupboard.

- ☐ Keep enough cash hidden away at home to cover family needs while you're away (and to give you cash for your wallet) in case you can't get to a bank or automatic teller machine.

Packing for All Occasions

Special Tip

If you are traveling with luggage that must be checked, pack the following into a carry-on bag or small suitcase on wheels:

☐ One set of underwear

☐ One pair of socks

☐ Pantyhose

☐ Travel slippers or beach shoes that can double as slippers

☐ Sleepwear

☐ Top

☐ Shorts

☐ Bathing suit

☐ Beach coverup; will double as bathrobe

☐ Slacks—if you're traveling in a skirt

☐ Skirt—if you're traveling in slacks

☐ Plastic raincoat or poncho

☐ Spare eyeglasses/contact lenses

☐ Sunglasses

☐ Cosmetic bag
☐ Foldable sun hat

If your luggage is misplaced or lost, you will be able to manage. You'll have two outfits—the one you wore for traveling, and your spare. You'll have your bathing suit (a difficult item to buy in a hurry on a trip). If you still have room in your carry-on, you can add more underwear and clothing and a pair of shoes.

What to Pack

☐ Select a few colors for your travel wardrobe. Some people find that black and white work well. Others prefer three colors—red, white, and blue, for example. This helps you narrow down your clothing choices. You can coordinate all your pieces and change the look with scarves and belts.

☐ Lay out the clothing you want to take, limiting yourself to the clothes in your color scheme. Choose nonwrinkle fabrics as much as possible.

☐ Pile blouses/tops together, pants together, etc.

☐ Take half of the items in each pile and put them back in the closet/drawer.

☐ Pack the remaining clothes.

☐ Select and pack a few scarves and belts to help you create new outfits.

☐ Pack light. Limit yourself to one suitcase. You'll appreciate not having too many pieces of luggage to handle and keep track of.

☐ For easy on-the-go laundering, bring along a few flat plastic hangers for drip drying over the tub, a small tube of cold-water laundry gel, and a small stain remover stick (or individual packets of stain remover).

☐ Include the following "life savers"—individual moist towelettes, travel-size packets of tissues, a raincoat or poncho, and a flashlight and batteries. Also, a rubber sink stopper is a must for contact-lens wearers. It's also helpful for hand washing in out-of-the-way places.

How to Pack

☐ Pack slacks and pants at the bottom of the suitcase. Fill in the corners with rolled-up belts and socks.

☐ Use plastic "zippered" bags to pack individual sets of underwear. These can also be used to fill corner spaces.

☐ Pack skirts so that the fold is at the sides. Pack dresses so the fold is at the waist.

☐ Use tissue paper to help avoid wrinkling clothes. Put a layer of tissue over each layer of clothing. Fill sleeves of jackets and dresses with tissue.

☐ Pack shoes in individual shoe bags or plastic or paper bags. Fit them in around the sides of the suitcase.

☐ Pack sport jackets and light coats on top. Pack heavy jackets and coats on top of slacks and pants.

☐ Make a list of every item in your suitcase. Keep a copy in the suitcase and a copy in your purse. You should also leave a copy at home.

☐ Have a nonremovable tag with your name printed clearly on each piece of luggage, including your carry-on bag.

Packing for Kids

☐ Have the child help select the travel wardrobe.

☐ Make room for a few small favorite items; for example, a stuffed animal, small doll, car, and a few books. These can go into a small carry-on bag that the child will hold and be responsible for.

☐ Pack complete outfits (shirt, pants, underwear, socks) into "zipper-top" plastic bags. This avoids a dressing crisis when a shirt is missing, and it makes decisions about what to wear a breeze.

☐ Have the child help you pack.

☐ Let the child make a list of what's in the suitcase.

☐ Make sure all special supplies are included—toiletries, spare eyeglasses, sunglasses, sun hat, etc.

☐ Keep a few new items—pocket games, books, pads and pencils—in your purse. Hand them out when boredom sets in.

Vacation Checklist

- ☐ Stop mail delivery; have mail held at the post office.
- ☐ Stop newspaper delivery.
- ☐ Hire someone to mow the lawn.
- ☐ Hire someone to shovel snow as needed.
- ☐ Put lights on timers. Have several lights on timers throughout the house.
- ☐ If you plan to retrieve telephone messages, leave your answering machine in operation. If you don't plan to retrieve messages, disconnect your machine.
- ☐ Give your itinerary to a friend or neighbor who will be able to reach you in an emergency. Also, give the person a key to your house.
- ☐ Notify your local police department; give them the name of the person who has your itinerary and the key to your house.
- ☐ Arrange for pet care. Select a kennel if necessary. If you are leaving your pet at home, hire someone to feed and exercise your pet. Be sure to leave an adequate supply of food. Leave the telephone number of the veterinarian.

□ Arrange to have your plants watered. If you will be away from home no longer than two weeks, you can safely leave your plants. Water them thoroughly before you leave; then cover them completely with plastic bags—plastic from dry cleaning is perfect for this. Make sure you cover the plants loosely; you're creating an air bubble that will keep moisture in and allow for circulation of air. There are also commercial long-term plant-feeding devices you can use.

□ Make sure your bills will be paid on time. Arrange to have pending bills paid or ask for extensions to avoid penalties.

Vacation-Equipment Checklist (Aside from Clothing)

☐ Passport/visas

☐ Airplane/train/bus tickets

☐ Itinerary

☐ Travelers' checks

☐ Travelers'-checks record

☐ Cash

☐ Credit card

☐ Travelers' insurance information

☐ Guidebooks/maps

☐ Address book or prepared labels

☐ Pen/pencil

☐ Travel journal/diary

☐ Camera equipment

☐ Film

☐ Camcorder cassettes

☐ Portable radio

☐ Portable cassette/CD player

☐ Cassettes/CDs

- ☐ Batteries
- ☐ Voltage adapter
- ☐ Electric shaver
- ☐ Hair dryer
- ☐ Books
- ☐ Flashlight
- ☐ Scissors
- ☐ Sewing/mending kit
- ☐ Umbrella
- ☐ Raincoat
- ☐ Medications and prescriptions
- ☐ Travel first-aid kit
- ☐ Eyeglasses and spare pair
- ☐ Contact lenses and spare pair
- ☐ Sunglasses and spare pair
- ☐ Sun hat
- ☐ Sunscreen/suntan lotion
- ☐ Toiletries
- ☐ Special equipment—skis, bicycle, golf clubs, tennis gear, camping gear, etc.

Travel Security Tips

☐ Make two copies of the first page of your passport. Leave one at home with other important papers. Take the other one with you and keep it separate from your passport—perhaps in your camera bag or other secured piece of luggage. Should your passport be lost or stolen, you will have the vital information you need to get a new one quickly. (Should you lose your copy, you can always call home for the important information you need.)

☐ If you plan on using a credit card, take only one. Choose a card that is universally accepted, and leave all other credit cards at home—in a secure place.

☐ Be careful with your travelers' checks. Follow instructions that come with the checks for recordkeeping and keeping track of your check numbers. It's a good idea to keep a duplicate set of records at home.

☐ Use a money belt for maximum security. Keep cash, passport, travelers' checks, and credit card in the belt. Select the style that is most comfortable for you—the shoulder "holster" style, the leg "holster" style, or the belt worn around the waist.

□ If your hotel offers the use of a safe or safety deposit box, take advantage of it and use it for all your valuables—your camera, binoculars, and such—as well as the obvious passport, cash, travelers' checks, jewelry. [Leave valuable jewelry at home in a safe or bank vault. Take only what you need to wear if attending a special event.]

□ Attach a sturdy luggage tag to each piece of luggage—even your carry-on. Do not include your street address—only your name and town. Put a label with your name and town on it inside each piece of luggage as well.

□ For easy identification, tie a distinctive colored ribbon to the handle of each piece of luggage. You'll be able to spot your bags easily as they roll around the baggage carousel.

□ If you use a backpack, wear it in front to keep pickpockets from opening pouches behind you when you're in a crowded area.

Tips for Traveling with a Young Child

Car Travel

☐ Make sure you use an approved safe and sturdy car seat. Strap your child in carefully so the child is seated correctly, with head and body supported properly.

☐ Protect your baby from exposure to sun; hang special sun-blocking shades on your side windows.

☐ Hang a mirror in back above the car seat so you can see your child in the rear-view mirror. There are unbreakable mirrors made especially for this purpose. Check your baby equipment store or mail order catalog.

☐ Have soft, safe toys for the baby to touch or look at; most car seats have room to attach them.

☐ Plan to take breaks to change and feed your baby.

Airplane Travel

☐ Notify the airline that you need to attach your car seat to the airline seat; or make sure the airline has the proper car seat for your baby to use.

☐ Make sure you and your baby are properly belted in; do not travel holding the baby on your lap or in your arms.

☐ If you have to change the baby, make sure that the "Fasten Seatbelts" sign is off.

☐ Airplane lavatories are often too small to change a baby in. You may have to use the seat. Don't forget to bring a large waterproof pad, along with the diapers and usual equipment.

☐ To avoid clogged ears on landing, have a pacifier or bottle at hand. Swallowing helps avoid ear discomfort or pain.

☐ Travel with a minimum of luggage; you'll have less of a wait if you can avoid checking your luggage. If you have a carriage, ask if you can stow it on the plane. Flight attendants often will have a special area for oversize equipment.

☐ If the plane isn't full, try to get an empty seat next to you so the child can lie down. Make sure the "Fasten Seatbelts" sign is off when having the child lie down on the seat.

☐ Bring along snacks and travel toys to keep the child busy. You could have a few special travel toys in a cloth bag; have the child reach in and pull one out to play with. Keep these for travel only, so they are always special.

121

Notes

Medical

Matters

I kill myself for my body.

First-Aid Kit Checklist

- ☐ First-aid booklet
- ☐ 1/2" adhesive-strip bandages
- ☐ 3/4" adhesive-strip bandages
- ☐ 1" adhesive-strip bandages
- ☐ 4" × 4" gauze pads
- ☐ Roll of flexible/stretch gauze
- ☐ Rolled bandages
- ☐ Roll of bandage tape
- ☐ Assorted nonstick sterile pads
- ☐ Triangular bandages
- ☐ Small splints
- ☐ Eye dressing/pads
- ☐ Scissors
- ☐ Tweezers
- ☐ Safety pins
- ☐ Disposable latex gloves
- ☐ Antiseptic ointment
- ☐ Antiseptic wipes
- ☐ Cold pack
- ☐ Pain relievers—aspirin or equivalent
- ☐ Ammonia inhalant
- ☐ Syrup of Ipecac

Emergency First-Aid Information

Call 911.

Note: The first-aid information provided here is for your general knowledge. It is *not* intended to replace first-aid instruction or professional medical advice. Seek professional help in any medical emergency. Doing the wrong thing is often worse than doing nothing at all. *Do not* attempt to provide help you are not qualified to administer.

First Aid for Choking: The Heimlich Maneuver

This has been accepted as the most effective method for dislodging an obstruction from the windpipe. Here are simple instructions to follow:

☐ Stand behind the person who's choking. If it's a child, you may have to kneel.

☐ Put your arms around the person's waist.

☐ Make a fist with one hand and place your thumb against the person's abdomen, just above the navel.

☐ Grasp your fist with your other hand. Position your fist in the middle of the person's abdomen.

125

☐ Press your fist into the person's abdomen with a quick, upward motion.

☐ Continue doing this at two-second intervals, until the object is dislodged.

Controlling Bleeding

☐ Apply pressure to the wound with a clean cloth. Bandage the wound to keep the pressure constant.

Burns

☐ Plunge the affected area into cold water immediately. Then apply ice. Keep ice on the burn until the pain subsides.

Master Medication List

Keep track of all the current medications your family is taking, along with the dosage of each. Record the prescription number as well, for easy reordering.

Name: _____

Medicine: _____

Dosage: _____

Prescription #: _____

Reason for taking medication: _____

Name: _____

Medicine: _____

Dosage: _____

Prescription #: _____

Reason for taking medication: _____

Name: _____

Medicine: _____

Dosage: _____

Prescription #: _____

Reason for taking medication: _____

MEDICAL MATTERS

Name: _____

Medicine: _____

Dosage: _____

Prescription #: _____

Reason for taking medication: _____

Name: _____

Medicine: _____

Dosage: _____

Prescription #: _____

Reason for taking medication: _____

Name: _____

Medicine: _____

Dosage: _____

Prescription #: _____

Reason for taking medication: _____

Name: _____

Medicine: _____

Dosage: _____

Prescription #: _____

Reason for taking medication: _____

Family Immunization Record

*Adult:*_____

Annual flu shot: _____

Tetanus shot: _____

Other: _____

Other: _____

Other: _____

*Adult:*_____

Annual flu shot: _____

Tetanus shot: _____

Other: _____

Other: _____

Other: _____

*Child:*_____

DPT:_____

Polio: _____

MMR: _____

Hepatitis B: _____

Other: _____

Other: _____

Other: _____

MEDICAL MATTERS

*Child:*_____

DPT:_____

Polio: _____

MMR: _____

Hepatitis B: _____

Other: _____

Other: _____

Other: _____

*Child:*_____

DPT:_____

Polio: _____

MMR: _____

Hepatitis B: _____

Other: _____

Other: _____

Other: _____

*Dog:*_____

Rabies: _____

Distemper: _____

Heartworm: _____

Lyme disease: _____

Bordatello: _____

*Dog:*_____

Rabies: _____

Distemper: _____

Heartworm: _____

Lyme disease: _____

Bordatello: _____

Cat: _____

Rabies: _____

Distemper (5 in 1): _____

Feline leukemia: _____

Feline infectious peritonitis (FIP): _____

Cat: _____

Rabies: _____

Distemper (5 in 1): _____

Feline leukemia: _____

Feline infectious peritonitis (FIP): _____

Family Health History

It's a good idea to keep track of all illnesses and conditions in your family. Some predispositions or conditions may be familial and may occur in each generation. Other medical conditions may skip a generation. It is also wise to keep a record of allergies—general and food or medication-specific. Include grandparents, parents, aunts and uncles, as well as siblings and children.

Name: _____ Age: _____
Chronic condition: _____
Past illnesses: _____
Surgery: _____
Allergies: _____
Food allergies: _____
Medication allergies: _____

Name: _____ Age: _____
Chronic condition: _____
Past illnesses: _____
Surgery: _____
Allergies: _____
Food allergies: _____
Medication allergies: _____

Name: _____ Age: _____
Chronic condition: _____
Past illnesses: _____
Surgery: _____
Allergies: _____
Food allergies: _____
Medication allergies: _____

Name: _____ Age: _____
Chronic condition: _____
Past illnesses: _____
Surgery: _____
Allergies: _____
Food allergies: _____
Medication allergies: _____

Name: _____ Age: _____
Chronic condition: _____
Past illnesses: _____
Surgery: _____
Allergies: _____
Food allergies: _____
Medication allergies: _____

MEDICAL MATTERS

Name: _____ Age: _____
Chronic condition: _____
Past illnesses: _____
Surgery: _____
Allergies: _____
Food allergies: _____
Medication allergies: _____

Name: _____ Age: _____
Chronic condition: _____
Past illnesses: _____
Surgery: _____
Allergies: _____
Food allergies: _____
Medication allergies: _____

Name: _____ Age: _____
Chronic condition: _____
Past illnesses: _____
Surgery: _____
Allergies: _____
Food allergies: _____
Medication allergies: _____

134

Name: _____ Age: _____
Chronic condition: _____
Past illnesses: _____
Surgery: _____
Allergies: _____
Food allergies: _____
Medication allergies: _____

Name: _____ Age: _____
Chronic condition: _____
Past illnesses: _____
Surgery: _____
Allergies: _____
Food allergies: _____
Medication allergies: _____

Name: _____ Age: _____
Chronic condition: _____
Past illnesses: _____
Surgery: _____
Allergies: _____
Food allergies: _____
Medication allergies: _____

Notes